"Finally, two public relations professionals have put together an easy-to-read, how-to media guide for industry representatives at all levels. AIA is to be commended for helping to make my job as a journalist easier."
– F. Clifton Berry, Jr.
Aerospace Editor, Author of Inventing The Future

"This is a bang-up, no-nonsense approach that can make dealing with the media a win-win situation. Both reporter and public relations professional, although coming from opposite directions, have the same objective – doing a credible job. This publication will help in preparation and ease the apprehension."
– Clarence A. Robinson, Jr.
Editor at Large, SIGNAL Magazine

"Business-media relations are adroitly covered in a book that belongs on every business bookshelf, *Media Isn't A Four Letter Word*, by veteran media-relations experts Dave J. Shea and John F. Gulick."
– Washington Business Journal

"A good primer and handy desktop reference for media relations pros can be found in the pages of *Media Isn't A Four Letter Word*."
– PR News

"When a reporter visits or telephones to do an interview about your company, try these techniques from public relations professionals David J. Shea and John F. Gulick."
– Marketing Briefing, Sussex, U.K.

"The legion of industry executives who cannot understand why their companies and their people often get what they view as bad press should give *Media Isn't A Four Letter Word* a long, thoughtful read."
— ***Richard C. Barnard***
Former Vice President, Executive Editor,
Defense News

"Media mavens David Shea and John Gulick have penned an extremely useful book that should be required reading for both reporters and those they cover."
— ***Defense Week***

"*Media Isn't* ... covers the essentials of media relations, including the dos and don'ts of press interviews, and pertinent comments from several working press people."
— ***O'Dwyer's PR Services Report***

"In *Media Isn't* ..., David Shea and John Gulick bequeath to their PR successors reasoned and time-proven advice for interacting with the media."
— ***Armed Forces Journal International LAURELS***

"When I saw the first edition of *Media Isn't* ..., it was a ray of sunshine. Finally, someone has presented a common-sense view of the media along with a few clear, simple and practical rules that help everyone on both sides of the pen and pad.
— ***David Silverberg***
Managing Editor, The Hill

Since first published in March 1994, *Media Isn't A Four Letter Word* has enjoyed remarkable success as a basic primer in understanding the ways and means of the working news media. Certainly, at the time of its initial publication by the Electronics Industries Alliance, the authors had little idea their views about media relations would be continued in a fifth edition, this one published by the Aerospace Industries Association. To both associations, the authors are extremely appreciative.

This new edition includes commentary from some of the most respected practitioners in the business. The foreword, by Mike McCurry, reflects his views on media relations as White House press secretary to President Bill Clinton in the mid-90s. David M. North, editor in chief of *Aviation Week & Space Technology,* combines his insight as both a journalist and pilot in the print media section of the book. Similarly, Pete Williams adds his perspective on dealing with the electronic media as both a former assistant secretary of defense for public affairs and network news correspondent for NBC Television News. Completing the new voices in the book are Howard Banks, long-time editor of *Forbes* magazine, who contributes his sage advice, along with unbiased perspectives from Rick Barnard, former editor of *Defense News,* and Robert T. Gilbert, a practicing public relations pro.

Over time, this book has evolved into a "must read" in the area of media relations and a respected adjunct in complementing corporate and government relations media training programs. In addition, the book's easy-to-understand advice and counsel have received critical acclaim from a number of national and international publications and well-known members of the news media. The authors gratefully acknowledge this professional acceptance and eagerly seek continued comments and suggestions to enhance future editions.

July 2002

MEDIA
ISN'T A FOUR LETTER
WORD

A GUIDE TO EFFECTIVE

ENCOUNTERS WITH THE

MEMBERS OF THE

FOURTH ESTATE

AEROSPACE INDUSTRIES
ASSOCIATION

By David J. Shea and John F. Gulick, APR

The Aerospace Industries Association of America Inc., based in Washington, D.C., is the premier trade association representing the nation's manufacturers of commercial, military and business aircraft helicopters, aircraft engines, missiles, spacecraft, materials and related components and equipment.

Founded in 1919, AIA speaks aggressively and effectively to convey industry goals and accomplishments and to voice common concerns to Congress, relevant federal agencies, international organizations, news media and the American public. The association provides a forum for industry and government to exchange views and resolve issues on non-competitive matters that relate to aerospace industries.

FIFTH EDITION, 2002

Managing Editor: Samantha Langley
Editors: Carol Jaka, Constance S. Moy, and B. Graham Simpson
Cover Design: Bryn Farrar
Layout: Mark Richards
Illustrations: Tony Frye

Library of Congress Cataloging-in-Publication Data

Gulick, John F.
  Media Isn't A Four Letter Word: A Guide to Effective Encounters with the
  Members of the Fourth Estate
Shea, David J.
  Media Isn't A Four Letter Word: A Guide to Effective Encounters with the
  Members of the Fourth Estate
p.   cm.
Originally published: Arlington, VA: EIA, 1994
ISBN: 0-9721132-0-7 $19.95
1. Media-Communications.   I.Title   II. Shea, David J.   III. Gulick, John F.
July 2002

TABLE OF CONTENTS

Far too often, industry executives in all disciplines equate a meeting with the news media with the same amount of anticipation and excitement as they would have for a root canal without anesthesia. However, by applying the proper anesthesia – such as training and preparation – they can turn a dreaded experience into a positive one.

As Thomas Jefferson wrote to John Jay in 1786, "Our liberty cannot be guarded but by the freedom of the press, nor that be limited without danger of losing it." The years may have changed, but these basic tenets have not.

INTRODUCTION
John W. Douglass

A free and open press, as Jefferson eloquently noted, is essential to the function of our democracy. Approached properly, a news media interview is a golden opportunity to educate your audience; in our case, we try to describe the critical role aerospace plays in our economy and in our overall national security. And given the challenges the aerospace industry faces today, we must be proactive and assume the responsibility to present the aerospace community's position so we may gain the public's trust, understanding and support.

Still, dealing with the media can be an intimidating experience for many industry executives. For that reason, the Aerospace Industries Association (AIA) has teamed with two public relations professionals — Dave Shea of Raytheon and John Gulick, most recently of Computer Sciences Corporation — to publish *Media Isn't A Four Letter Word.* I hope you find their advice and counsel of timely assistance in helping you to navigate through potential media minefields. This book has a proud heritage, and AIA is pleased to continue that legacy by making it available in this fifth edition.

John W. Douglass
President and CEO
Aerospace Industries Association

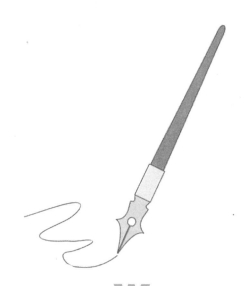

AUTHORS' NOTE

When we set out in early 1994 to write a how-to guide for dealing effectively with the news media, times were certainly different. Today we are faced — thanks to the World Wide Web and the proliferation of media outlets — with an insatiable appetite for 24/7 news. This naturally has been exacerbated by the events and emotions surrounding September 11, 2001.

Deadlines are now. Competition among the news media to be first with the story, if not necessarily right, is fierce. More than ever, business executives must take the time to become "media savvy."

Helping the media to get the story right isn't solely the province of company or association spokespeople. It's also the job of subject matter experts, executives at all managerial levels, program managers and others, up to and including a company's chairman, CEO and members of the board of directors.

We recognize that many have valid concerns about talking to reporters, and we are not suggesting that you must like the media as an institution. We are emphatically asserting, however, that to be successful in today's competitive environment, a business must conduct a meaningful media relations program. To ignore the media's obvious and immediate impact on today's business world can be suicidal. Certainly the lessons of the Exxon *Valdez*, Three Mile Island and, more recently, Enron and Arthur Andersen LLP quickly come to mind.

Once you get started, working with the media becomes a challenge, somewhat akin to riding a bicycle for the first time. Yes, you probably will fall off a time or two, but once you've done it and gained some confidence, future trips will be that much more uneventful and, as Mike McCurry alludes to in his foreword, quite possibly rewarding.

Remember, though, when the media calls, don't try to do it all by yourself. Trust the professional counsel of your organization's public relations/media relations team. This is their beat. There is nothing to be gained by trying to out-think or sidestep these pros when you need them most. Listen to them and heed their advice. That's the reason you hired them in the first place.

Indeed, *Media Isn't...* isn't designed to replace your professional PR staff. Rather, our work here — as it was in our first edition — is to capture in one concise, easy-to-use reference the techniques and tips essential to building confidence when you are called upon to do a media interview.

We wish to acknowledge the encouragement and support of several individuals who have stepped up to ensure *Media Isn't...* continues to see the light of day. Thanks go to Phyllis J. Piano, vice president, Corporate Affairs and Communications, Raytheon Company; Steven Van Horn, vice president, Technology Management Group, Computer Sciences Corporation; Alexis Allen, AIA's enthusiastic director of communications; and Ceil Wloczewski and her highly competent graphics staff at CSC's P2 Communications Services.

We also acknowledge and thank our media relations colleagues for their valuable comments and suggestions, many of which are incorporated into this latest edition.

We particularly appreciate the contribution of our Raytheon colleague Paul Stefens, who has been dealing with the news media in Europe, the Middle East and Africa for decades. Our treatment of international media is based principally on his experience.

And finally, our sincerest thanks go to the members of the working media for their instructive and pithy comments. It is comforting to realize that at least within the context of this book, we are on the same page. A listing of the media members who have contributed to *Media Isn't ...* is found in Appendix F.

Dave Shea and John Gulick
Washington, D.C.

Rats! I was all stoked up to write the definitive treatise on how you, too, can survive daily encounters with the news media and live to tell the tale when I came across this nifty volume by David J. Shea and John F. Gulick. I'm not sure there is anything left to say. The authors have captured about all the good advice there is and packaged it in this easy-to-read, simple-to-understand guide to working with the news media.

The important thing is the way the authors demystify the press. Understanding reporters and how they think and do their work is vital. Many industry executives seem to think that press relations is voodoo. They often encounter the press with a look that suggests they are getting stuck with a pin.

FOREWORD
Mike McCurry

A reporter approaches any source from a skeptical, adversarial point of view. Reporters like to think they are the last defense between a pack of lies and the public, so they usually go about their jobs with an *attitude*. That puts off a lot of folks in business and politics, and they never get to the point where they can deal politely and professionally with the press.

Look, you don't have to like the press. You do need to understand that they are doing a job, they take their work seriously and they have their own (largely unwritten) set of professional standards. Understanding their rules of the road, their terms of art and the dos and don'ts of reporting makes you better prepared to approach the reporter on his or her terms. In short, the relationship between you and the press is designed to be adversarial. That doesn't mean it has to be less than amicable.

The authors of *Media Isn't A Four Letter Word* know exactly the barriers that stand in the way of effective communication. This book shows how to tear those barriers down and turn an adversarial relationship between reporter and source into a more balanced, healthy one.

To my own mind, the rules, tips and techniques set out here boil down to what I often call the "Mike McCurry Five C's of Effective Press Relations":

Credibility. You can only lose sight of the truth once before you lose the ability to deal in an honest, straightforward manner with the press. In my career, ahem, this lesson has often been learned the hard way. The press trusts and likes straight shooters, and they go back to those sources that provide good, factual, accurate information.

Candor. A corollary to credibility, candor requires the communicator to acknowledge errors, 'fess up to mistakes and handle the bad stories along with the good. The press appreciates folks who don't try bizarre attempts at "spin" when something has been fouled up. This is hard for many in business and politics, where the temptation is usually to try and put a silver gloss on the darkest clouds.

Clarity. Yes, we are stupid, and yes, we should keep it simple. In truth, we are all busy and overwhelmed and there is too much information floating around in this world of instantaneous global communications. Only precise and sharply defined messages stand out in the blur of information overload. The best piece of advice in this book is to write down on a piece of paper a simple one-sentence statement that captures the essence of what you are trying to say.

Compassion. Having some empathy for the poor, overworked and underpaid reporter and understanding his or her pressures or deadlines goes a long way to putting some human balance into the adversarial relationship. Listening carefully to the questions, understanding and being polite to critics and naysayers, and avoiding snarls at the persistent interviewer all help make a difficult job easier to handle, for both the reporter and the communicator.

Commitment. Organizations need to treat communications seriously. The function needs a good budget and good people, and it is imperative that those people work at the very top of the organization chart. They have to have good access to the executives and information that make the enterprise go. Good media and public relations is a bottom-line activity, and good executives today are giving this part of their business a great deal more attention.

Now I have coughed up all my secrets, and there are none left to publish. Thanks to the AIA and to David Shea and John Gulick, no one can say they haven't been well-armed in the combat that often is "media relations." If you are well-armed, you might even enjoy your encounters with members of the fourth estate. Try it; you just might like it.

Mike McCurry is chairman and CEO, Grassroots Enterprise Inc. He is a veteran political strategist and spokesperson with 25 years' experience in Washington, D.C. He served in the White House as press secretary to President Bill Clinton (1995 – 1998), spokesman for the Department of State (1993 – 1995) and director of communications for the Democratic National Committee (1988 – 1990). He holds a bachelor's degree from Princeton University and a master's from Georgetown University.

"The executive who learns how to deal with the press well becomes an invaluable resource to his or her company."

Jack Sweeney
Consulting Magazine

"The rise of ambush TV has made things more difficult on all levels of journalism. Remember though, that the vast majority of reporters will deal with you fairly and honestly. Talking to them is a crucial part of doing business."

Peter Grier
Christian Science Monitor

PREPARING FOR A MEDIA INTERVIEW

CHAPTER 1

Whether you're a low handicapper or weekend hacker, hitting a bucket of balls prior to playing golf can help prepare you for the pain or pleasures that lie ahead. Much the same can be said when preparing for a media interview. Preparation is paramount.

BEFORE YOU ACCEPT

What should you know and evaluate before deciding to participate in an interview?

Assuming you are the right person to do the interview (if not, don't hesitate to say so), consider the following questions before agreeing to it:

■ Is there a compelling reason not to speak publicly on the subject in question? For example, does the information or subject area border on company proprietary, sensitive, restricted or even classified information? Are there political or policy concerns?

■ If the information or subject matter deals with a government contract, does your government customer want or expect you to discuss the contract publicly? If you're a subcontractor, what is the prime contractor's position? If you're not sure, talk with your procurement and public relations staffs and determine the proper course of action.

- What is the scope of the reporter's interest? Where is the story going? Is there a hidden agenda? Having at least a basic understanding of the reporter's story line should help you formulate your answers.

- Has the correspondent/publication/network reported on this subject before? If so, what was the slant of the story? Positive? Critical? Neutral?

- What's the reporter's reputation for accuracy and balance? How familiar is he or she with the subject matter?

- Are you the sole individual being interviewed for the story, or are there others? (It's OK to ask the reporter.)

"Rarely do great interviews just happen – they're the product of diligent preparation on both sides of the table. On the industry side, both the PR rep and the person being interviewed should have a clear understanding of where they'd like the interview to go long before the tape recorder rolls."

John Roos
Armed Forces Journal International

■ If you've determined that the story may be negative or controversial, do you have more to gain or lose by being interviewed? This is always a tough call and must be made on a case-by-case basis. Generally, unless you speak up — controversy notwithstanding — your company or association's position will not be heard and will be conspicuously missing from the story. In short, your absence means you concede the article or broadcast to your critics. In other words, dealing with the media is akin to playing baseball. If you don't show up, you forfeit the game.

■ Where and how will the interview be conducted? When dealing with a print reporter, try to do the interview in person rather than over the phone. This format usually allows you to communicate more effectively. In today's hectic world, however, the phone interview is becoming the norm, so grab the opportunity regardless.

■ How much time is needed for the interview? Most print interviews take 30 to 45 minutes. In-depth reporting may require more time. So be flexible.

■ What are the interview ground rules? Establish them up front before accepting the interview. Most importantly, be sure that all participants understand the rules you set. More on this in Chapter 2.

Answering these questions will help you appropriately decide whether to be interviewed. In most instances, it is better to seize the opportunity to get your company or association's performance on the record. Start with the proposition that the media is a conduit to audiences vitally important to your business interests. Consider the press as a resource. If, on the other hand, you decline the request, be prepared to explain why.

GETTING READY

Don't go into a media interview cold. Preparation is key.

■ If possible, research what the reporter has written. In the case of the electronic media, watch/ listen to the reporter or news program requesting the interview. With print media, obtain copies of previous stories through an electronic, online or news clipping service (your PR department can help you with this). Even if the stories don't deal directly with the pending subject, they should give you some insight into the reporter's approach and style.

■ If you are one of several people contributing to the same story, talk with the others and compare notes.

- Try to anticipate the questions: the good, the bad and the ugly. After all, you know the subject and should know how to address all areas, including those you would prefer to avoid. Be prepared for the negative questions and, together with your PR counsel, prepare your responses.

- Scan the general media and trade press before your interview. Don't be caught off guard by late-breaking events that might bear on the topic.

- Gather supporting material ahead of time. (You don't need to carry everything in your head.) It helps to have white papers or fact sheets to which both you and the reporter can refer during the interview. If the print or radio interview is by phone, offer to e-mail or fax the material. Don't forget photos (or video — Beta SP or 3/4 inch — for TV) or other art-work that might help you tell your story. Frequently,

" We in the media are writing things that may not necessarily be pleasant for everyone involved. It's nothing personal. It's the business. "

Vargo Muradian
Defense News

good visuals can determine whether your viewpoint is included. But remember, if you quote from or use background information in front of a reporter, be prepared to provide that material if asked. A good rule of thumb: If you don't want the reporter to have it, don't show or bring it to the interview.

■ If an interview deals with a particularly sensitive or troublesome subject, consider preparing by using a "murder board." In this exercise, your PR people play the role of reporters and grill you with questions — both easy and tough — on the interview subject. It's also a good idea to videotape and/or audiotape the session so you can discuss your performance and reshape (or research) your answers, if needed, before the actual interview.

DEVELOPING YOUR MESSAGES

Prepare for all interviews by developing your own agenda. In fact, go into every interview knowing precisely what you'd like to see in print or on the air. In other words, if you could write the lead for the article, what would it be? How do you do this? Simple: Develop message points.

Before the interview, identify three, four or five main points you want the reporter to take from the interview. These are your key messages, your "commercials." Keeping these messages in mind should help you guide and control the interview. Write your messages on 3- by 5-inch cards and refer to them as the interview progresses. Your messages should be clear, easily understood assertions or facts that can be independently verified.

> **"** *Industry officials should keep in mind that if they are unwilling to talk to the media, someone else will.* **"**
>
> *John Moore*
> *Information*
> *Technology Writer*

For example, if you work for a company defending against charges of pollution, you could say, "We're a safe company and concerned about the environment." But you would increase your credibility with the viewers and readers if you backed up your claim:

> *Safety is our number one concern. During our 35-year history, as government environmental records will show, we've never had a spill. Our employees, from top management down, receive 90 hours of annual training. This far exceeds the industry average. We're proud to have been recognized as one of the safest companies in the state last year. That's an honor we hope to receive every year.*

OK, so you've done your homework and are now prepared to do the actual interview. If you remember nothing else, please remember these two cardinal rules:

- If you don't want to see it in print or hear it on the air, don't say it!

- Engage brain before putting mouth in gear!

Remembering these two simple rules up front can save you and your organization a great deal of pain and suffering later on.

> **" While it's OK to ask a reporter for the subject areas to be discussed during an interview, never ask for the specific questions in advance. And if you're unsure as to how much he or she knows about the subject, offer to provide facts and data ahead of time. "**
>
> **Carl Rochelle
> Former
> Correspondent, CNN**

*David North has
been an editor at*
Aviation Week &
Space Technology
*for the past 26 years,
covering most
aspects of the aero-
space industry. He
served as managing
editor for eight years
prior to assuming
his present position
as editor in chief in
1996. He has served
as both a carrier-
based U.S. Navy
attack pilot and as a
pilot/flight engineer
for Pan American
World Airways.
North graduated
from the U.S. Naval
Academy and has a
master's degree in
communication
theory from RPI in
Troy, N.Y.*

From the Journalistic Left Seat
*By David M. North, Editor in Chief
Aviation Week & Space Technology*

I doubt very many aerospace officials ever took "How
to Deal With the News Media" as a credit course in
college. But once individuals reach certain levels
of managerial responsibility, they will be required to
know how to deal with the press. It behooves everyone to take time to understand the personalities,
process and expected outcome from meetings with
members of the fourth estate. Having a realistic
understanding of the journalist's role will help the
editorial process and, in the long term, help ensure
an accurate and balanced story.

There are many professional public relations people
walking the halls of industry, and I have worked
with many of them for years. For the most part, they
know how to present information and develop good
relations with the media. Executives should listen
to their advice and counsel, lest they do themselves
and their organization a disservice.

I came to journalism more than 25 years ago via
engineering and my duties as a military and commercial pilot. While my experience certainly has shaped
my impressions as to whether a company executive
or military officer may be attempting to stonewall
or bluff me on facts, or that a problem is not as grave
as it appears, I suspect my reactions are not much
different from those of my professional colleagues.
My point is that our varying experience levels enable
us to draw the line of credibility at different points
on the scale.

As a journalist, I have specific reasons for conducting an interview. Usually it is to determine whether there is a story sitting opposite me. I then need to determine whether that story is positive or negative and is something I need to write about now or later. At *Aviation Week & Space Technology,* our focus usually is on what is "going" to happen. My goal is to recount the problem, then tell the reader how that problem is likely to be resolved. As an editor of a news magazine, I do not normally include extensive amounts of history in my stories. My intent is to report the story in a balanced, accurate and timely way.

On the positive side, anything you can do to help me do my job only works to get your story out in the best possible manner. Be truthful. A straightforward approach to the issues and facts is always best. If you have graphs, charts or photographs to make your points, let me see them. They can help any journalist present a more understandable and compelling story.

On the negative side, don't tell me "no comment," or I will only look harder for the reason why. While I might be temporarily deceived — and the initial story may reflect that — the truth will come out, and you simply will not be trusted again. Running that risk, especially in a particularly close-networked environment like aerospace and defense, can be costly. If you cannot divulge a certain fact or intent because of proprietary or competitive reasons or do not know the answer, tell me. I'll understand and respect you for your candor. Trying to dance around or bluff

your way through an answer will only create larger
and more pervasive problems over time.

Do not be deceived. Reporters and editors are not
your friends in the traditional sense of the word.
Our relationship is correctly defined as adversarial.
And that's why it works. I have a periodic discussion with a top aerospace executive who constantly
chides me and my staff about why we're not more
positive boosters of aerospace. "You should write
nothing that could hurt the industry," he tells me.
His rationale is misguided.

While most of us love things that fly through the air
— and especially when pulling "g's" in a supersonic
new fighter at 30,000 feet — we are professional
journalists first. And if we uncover wrongdoing,
stupidity, a budget overrun or delayed schedules,
we are going to write about it. The industry and its
global participants deserve nothing less.

CHAPTER 2

Whether a print interview is by phone or in person,

a representative from your PR department should sit

in to protect you and your company's interests. Don't

be embarrassed to tape record the interview; after all,

that's exactly what many reporters do to ensure accu-

racy. Your actions should be no different. The tape

provides a record of what was said and the context in

which the discussion occurred. Certainly, a reporter who uses a tape recorder is less likely to misquote a source. (Note: If, for security reasons, your company prohibits tape recorders on its premises, be sure to advise the reporter ahead of time.)

After the opening amenities (including an exchange of business cards to ensure the reporter gets your name and title right), the PR advisor should establish the ground rules. (If no PR representative is present, the honor falls to you.) This discussion should be on tape as well. We can't stress enough how important it is to agree on the ground rules at the outset to avoid misunderstanding and embarrassment later.

GROUND RULES

Ground rules are exactly that – a set of rules that establish the framework of how the interview will be conducted and reported. Whether you may or may not be quoted by name and title, or whether the information you provide may or may not be attributed to you or your company are examples of ground rules.

While there may be variations in the terms, here are generally accepted definitions of the terms used in setting ground rules:

■ *On the Record:* This is perhaps the most common and recommended ground rule. In an on-the-record interview, the reporter may use all the information you provide and attribute it directly to you by name, title and organization.

> **"** *Whenever I see a PR rep introducing him/herself to the prospective interviewee, I know it's going to be an interesting session.* **"**
>
> *John Roos*
> *Armed Forces*
> *Journal*
> *International*

■ ***Background:*** In a background interview, you may not be identified by name. There are variations to the background interview that may be used as appropriate: simple background, background on a not-for-attribution basis and deep background.

• *Simple Background*: There may be sound reasons why you do not wish to be quoted by name. Fine. But, in these instances, it may make sense to be identified by your company or association name. For example, "The AIA reported today that aerospace sales during the first quarter of 2001 ..." or "According to Computer Sciences Corporation, the practice of awarding best value contracts in the federal government is ... ."

In any event, agree at the outset as to how you will be identified, for example, as a Raytheon official, a CSC executive, an association vice president, etc.

• *Not for Attribution:* In this type of interview, you may neither be quoted by name nor identified by title, company or association. Generally, remarks made here are attributed to "an industry source." Again, agree at the outset how you will be referred to in the article.

• *Deep Background:* This form of background interview isn't often used because it's just a shade above off the record. In a deep background interview, what you say may be used, but only without any attribution whatsoever. The resulting article will contain no hint that the reporter received your assistance. You may wish to use deep background to help a reporter understand past events or avoid errors.

■ ***Off the Record:*** The reporter may not use any of the information you provide. A word of caution: Do this type of interview rarely, if at all. You may be embarrassed if the ground rule is unintentionally or intentionally broken.

If you feel you must go off the record, do so only if you know the reporter extremely well and if what you have to say is crucial to the reporter's understanding of complex factors involved in the story.

One last critical point: Never provide information first and then tell the reporter the ground rule that applied, such as, "That's off the record." Guess what? It isn't, and it wasn't. It's only off the record when the reporter agrees to accept information as off the record before you give it.

Make it a policy not to switch ground rules during the course of an interview. Although on occasion it may be necessary, going from on the record to background to off the record and back only leads to confusion.

TECHNIQUES

Now let's examine some techniques for conveying your points clearly, accurately and forcefully, and how you can try to control and influence an interview.

■ *Last Things First:* The most effective way to make your point is to answer a question with your conclusions or main points first, then reinforce with facts. This is known as headlining. It's akin to the inverted pyramid format of a news story, starting from the general and moving to the specific.

For example, if you were asked to explain the recent test failures of the Boomerang missile, you might respond, "At 85 percent, the Boomerang enjoys the highest success rate of any missile tested to date. Despite some recent setbacks, we have great confidence in it. ..." In other words,

> **"***Don't pitch me a story unless you know that it's something I cover. There are few things more frustrating than wasting time on misdirected pitches and then being asked to suggest someone else you can talk to. It's not my responsibility to help you get your pitch into the paper.***"**
>
> **Karen Kaplan**
> **Los Angeles Times**

stress the positives first, then back them with explanatory facts.

■ *Telegraph Your Main Points:* Use forceful phrases such as, "The real issue here is ..." or "Key to our success has been ..." or "Don't ever forget that ... ." This highlighting technique signals that your priority messages are about to be delivered — kind of like the college professor and his "foot stomping" main points right before the big test.

■ *If You Don't Like the Question, Answer Your Own:* This is called bridging. Politicians have literally turned it into an art form. If you get a question that doesn't pertain to your agenda, briefly touch on it and quickly move or "bridge" to a topic or point more germane to your message.

For example, if asked whether your program is in trouble on the Hill, say, "There are some honest differences of opinion in Congress over the future of the Boomerang, but we enjoy solid support in the Air Force and DoD. Let me tell you why." This is your bridge to discuss the support the Boomerang program is receiving.

■ *Rephrase Negative Questions:* If you're uncomfortable with how a question is asked, rephrase it. Then provide an answer. For example, "With the Bravo and Bolo missiles already in the inventory, isn't the Boomerang unnecessary and duplicative?" Begin your response with, "I believe what you're really getting at is what makes the Boomerang unique. ..." Rephrasing not only removes a negative, but also creates a more comfortable situation in which you can respond with your positive points.

❝You have a right to know what kind of story the reporter is working on. What's the context for the interview? Try to determine where the reporter is coming from. Most journalists will be quite open about that.❞

Peter Grier
Christian Science
Monitor

Remember: Don't repeat the negative key words in a question. As songwriter Johnny Mercer wrote years ago, "Accentuate the positive, eliminate the negative."

■ ***Watch the "If" Word:*** Be extremely careful when asked a hypothetical question. When "if" is in the question, alarm bells should ring. It's always safer to stick to the facts and forgo supposition, unless it's part of your strategy. For example, if you consciously wish to get on the public record the impact of a 20 percent cut in congressional funding, then answer the "what if." For example, you could say, "If there's a cut, then we'd have a break in production and not achieve operational status on time." However, be sure you want to see that projection reported, because it will be.

If, on the other hand, you don't want to answer the question, respond accordingly: "I'd prefer not to speculate on what Congress may do."

■ *Watch Your Language:* Avoid jargon as much as possible. Don't assume the reporter knows what "TRACON,"
"SBIRS" or "JDAM" mean.* If you do, you'll probably
create confusion, and the reporter will miss your point. If
you absolutely feel you have to use acronyms, make sure
you define them the first time around.

Speaking of language, careful, quotable and colorful
phrases usually will find their way into print or onto
the air. But try to come up with these ahead of time.
A shot from the hip can hit you in the foot. Use
examples and anecdotes. They help write or tell the
story. Be especially cautious when attempting to be
funny. An innocent humorous aside can make a great
– but embarrassing – quote.

■ *Don't Be Gratuitous:* Try to answer each question
completely and truthfully, but be careful about volunteering information unless it supports a positive point. For

> **❝**Reporters on
> deadline need their
> calls returned quickly.
> *If you're unable to*
> *call back, have some-*
> *one else do it for you.*
> *Don't let phone mes-*
> *sages linger until a*
> *reporter's frustration*
> *boils over.* **❞**
>
> *Larry Margasak*
> *Associated Press*

*These terms stand for "Terminal Radar Approach Control Facility," "Space-Based
Infrared System" and "Joint Direct Attack Munition."

example, if asked the status of the Boomerang, it may be perfectly appropriate to recite a long list of facts. But to go on to say that certain military tests are unnecessary or that program plans may change spells headlines — usually the kind you don't want. Rule of thumb: Answer the question and only the question. Be careful about speaking for third parties, be they customers, suppliers or Congress, unless you have cleared it with them ahead of time.

■ *Make Your Point:* What if the topic or points you'd like to discuss don't come up during the interview? Simple! Bring them up yourself. Don't be shy about getting your messages across. Frequently, at the end of an interview a reporter might ask, "Is there anything else I should have asked or we didn't cover?" Here's your chance to knock the ball out of the park. Even if you've already covered all your major points, take the opportunity to summarize and highlight your messages again.

If a reporter's question stumps you, don't be afraid to say so. A simple, "I don't know the answer to that, but I'll get back to you" builds not only credibility, but also positive relationships. No one expects you to know all the answers off the top of your head, so don't bluff. If you indicate you will provide follow-up material, make sure you know the reporter's deadline and deliver on time. You can't influence a story once its deadline has passed.

Three more points. First, the interview isn't over until it's over, that is, when you or the reporter has left the scene. Don't let your guard down just because the tape recorder has been turned off or the pen has been capped. The interview is over only when the reporter, camera person, sound technician and whoever has left the room are escorted from and off your facility and are in their cars heading down the highway.

Second, although a reporter may occasionally volunteer to let you review technical aspects of a story prior to publication, never ask. At best it's considered bad form, and at worst it's an insult. Many publications have a rule against outsiders reviewing stories before they're published.

Third, a reporter is a reporter 24 hours a day, not just during formal interviews. You run the risk of being a "news source" any time you talk with a member of the media, whether it's in your office, at the club playing golf or chatting in the mall parking lot on a Saturday afternoon.

Facing the Camera? Don't Sweat It; You're in Control

By Pete Williams, NBC Television News

First of all, less of what you say in an interview will appear in a TV story than in a newspaper story. The average print story might use several sentences, quoted directly, throughout the story. The television story will usually use just one or two sections of the interview, or "sound bites."

That gives the interview subject less of a chance to get the point across in a TV story, making it all the more important to have a theme in mind.

When I interview someone, particularly an expert, I am actually rooting for that person. I become their ally, in a sense, because I want the interview subject to succeed for the sake of my story. I want that expert to look good on the air and to make a solid contribution to my story. So I might actually ask a question several times, phrasing it in different ways, to elicit the best possible answer – one that is brief but packs a punch. My advice to interviewees?

– Give the subject some thought before the camera arrives. Think up a key phrase or two and build your answers around them.

– Practice. Before the TV crew arrives, practice saying the answers out loud. Rehearse in front of a colleague to get the hang of making your point to a listener. If possible, have someone ask the question so that you can respond. Don't just think about it. Say it. But don't overdo it. Obviously rehearsed or canned answers look flat and dull and won't make it on the air.

Prior to joining NBC, Pete Williams served on Capitol Hill in a number of media liaison roles. He served as press secretary and legislative assistant to then-Congressman Dick Cheney in 1986 and was appointed assistant secretary of defense for public affairs when Cheney was named secretary of defense in 1989. Williams is a graduate of Stanford University and was named Government Communicator of the Year in 1991 by the National Association of Government Communicators.

— Be brief. Most television sound bites are a sentence or two, ranging from around six to 14 seconds. Impossibly brief? Not at all. Most of history's most memorable quotes are about that length. Local stations will use some longer snippets, but network sound bites tend to be somewhat shorter. Most of the quotes in newspaper stories are about that length, too.

— The best sound bites offer opinion or reveal emotion. When I write a TV story, I prefer to handle the details, summarizing the chronological narrative, adding up the numbers and percentages or noting the historical context. That leaves it to the interview subjects to explain what this information means or to give their opinions on an event's significance. If the story is a new invention, the reporter will most likely explain how it works and will delve into the technical details. The interview would be used to elicit the inventor's view of why the invention is important or how it will make things better.

— Finally, remember that you're in control. If you don't understand a question, ask the interviewer to rephrase it. Answer only the questions you understand. The TV reporter cannot put on the air the answer you don't give. That gives you all the power. You say only what you want to say. So don't sweat it. You're in control.

THE BROADCAST MEDIA INTERVIEW

CHAPTER 3

Surveys consistently show that the majority of people get most of their news from TV and radio, i.e., the broadcast or electronic media. So, unless there are compelling reasons not to do so, join the 21st century and seize the electronic opportunity.

Many of the techniques for successful print interviews may also be applied to radio and TV. However,
the broadcast media presents its own unique require-
ments and challenges.

All broadcast stories have one thing in common:
brevity. You have to recognize up front that collect-
ing and researching the electronic story may take
hours, but only a small percentage of that information will make it on the air. A spot news item will
typically run from 15 to 90 seconds. A feature story
usually runs longer, maybe two to four minutes. In
either case, that's not a lot of time to get your points
across. But this does not have to inhibit you when
dealing with the electronic media.

■ *Speak in Sound Bites:* Respond with concise
answers. Put key points up front. Avoid jargon. You
have to learn to speak in "sound bites." Respond with
answers that don't run over 15 seconds. Briefer is

better. You can do it. It just takes a little practice. (Notice how short these sentences are.) It's the old story: Tell the time, don't build a watch.

TELEVISION

Preparation is the key to success in all interviews, but especially a TV interview. Whether you are an integral part of a news story or a guest on an interview program, certain basic principles apply.

- *Give Yourself Time:* If a news crew is coming to your office, select a suitable area to conduct the interview. Avoid windows and other areas that might reflect light. Don't use a room with fluorescent lighting and be prepared to turn off the overhead lights if asked. Use the crew's setup time to discuss the area of questioning with the reporter. Don't allow the camera to roll until you're ready. Remember, the interview is on your turf.

❝ With print reporters, you can ramble on. TV is looking for a sound bite. It needs to be succinct; it can't be 35 or 40 seconds. The ideal is a 15- to 20-second bite that makes your point in layman's terms. ❞

Carl Rochelle
Former
Correspondent, CNN

If it's a studio interview, arrive early to check your appearance, familiarize yourself with the set — camera positions, monitors, etc. — and go over the line of questioning.

■ *Taped Versus Live Shows:* If you are being interviewed one-on-one on tape for later broadcast, you do have some latitude. For example, if you feel you are not responding as well as you could to a particular question, or you left out a vital piece of information, stop and start over. The reporter won't care. Keep in mind, the reporter has his or her reputation on the line as well. Most reporters are just as interested in a professional and timely news report as you are.

On the other hand, if a program is live or being taped for broadcast within a certain time allocation, you won't have the luxury to stop and go back. What you say is what you get.

You should be aware that TV stations in smaller markets may send only one individual to cover an interview, event or activity. In these situations, that individual is the camera person, sound technician, setup person and the on-camera interviewer talent. This means there can be only one camera position at a time, so don't be surprised if the reporter wants to do what are called "cut-aways" following the completion of an interview. These scenes are essential so the reporter — in the edited interview — can cut between interviewee and interviewer to achieve a smooth question and answer format.

> **❝** *Television news always prefers the top dog. If that's not possible, send only a PR person to go on camera who is empowered with the facts and prepared to respond for you and your company.* **❞**
>
> **Tim White**
> **Television Journalist and Producer**

■ ***"How" Is as Important as "What":*** A wag once said that TV journalism is to journalism as TV dinners are to dinner. Whether or not you agree, TV is the prime source of people's impressions. Since TV is a visual medium, what you say is frequently judged by how you say it and how you look when you say it.

Some experts believe that of the total message presented on TV, seven percent is what you say, 38 percent is how you say it and 55 percent is non-verbal communication.

During a one-on-one interview, for example, look directly at the reporter. Forget about the camera. Concentrate on what he or she is saying. Looking into the air or at the floor or darting your eyes back and forth distracts the viewer and makes you look evasive, distrustful and unsure of yourself. Remember to stay involved, even when you aren't speaking or on camera.

■ *Language:* As previously discussed, avoid jargon and acronyms. This is especially true with the electronic media since there isn't time to go back or define your terms. If you want to talk about the National Performance Review, then call it that and forget "NPR." After all, that's National Public Radio. Right?

Try to respond with simple, direct sentences. If an answer involves technical information, include it but follow with an appropriate explanation.

Focus on statements that will grab the audience's attention. If possible, be ready with concrete examples, meaty quotes and positive answers to tough questions. Be careful with numbers since they tend to get lost. Rather than saying, "79 out of 98 tests were successful," say, "Approximately 80 percent hit the mark."

■ **Body Language:** Avoid obvious signs of nervousness such as rapid eye blinking, foot tapping, clenched fists, crossed arms, frowning, shifting back and forth during a stand-up interview and jingling pocket change.

Use small gestures (remember, most directors go for closeups) and animated facial expressions to emphasize

> **"***As an industry official, you should view a TV interview request as an opportunity to make your case. If you don't participate, then you have no influence over the outcome of the story.***"**
>
> **Carl Rochelle**
> **Former**
> **Correspondent, CNN**

a point. Don't hold a pencil or pen or any other object that you might fiddle with while on camera. You may not even know you are doing it. But both the camera and the microphone will record it.

■ **Posture:** If it's a stand-up interview, stand up straight. Don't rock or sway. Keep your head up.

During a sit-down interview, sit close to the edge of your chair with your back straight. If you are wearing a suit coat, sit on the coattails so your jacket doesn't bunch up at the neck. Take your elbows off the chair arms. Take deep breaths, both to relax and to retain enough air to finish a thought.

■ **Long Pauses:** A technique used by some TV reporters is to pause at the end of your answer. They hope you'll think you haven't adequately responded and will feel obligated to keep on talking.

Don't take the bait. Smile and remain confident in your answer. Answer the question and only the question.

Speaking of pauses, there is no need to jump right in after the interviewer finishes his or her question. Take a second or two to gather your thoughts. This enables the editors to make clean edits. And, if you get a tough or sensitive question, phrases such as, "I'm glad you asked me that," or "That is really a key question" can give you a few seconds to collect your thoughts and formulate your answer.

■ *Attitude:* Nothing comes through more obviously on TV than a hostile or arrogant attitude. Be cool. Be natural. Be pleasant. Be sincere. Be animated. And above all, be truthful.

> **"** *The failure of any executive to speak with the press raises the suspicions of any good reporter. The reporter may dig harder and start speaking to the executive's underlings. I love speaking to underlings.* **"**
>
> *Jack Sweeney*
> *Consulting*
> *Magazine*

Once again, *the interview isn't over until it's over.* That is, when the camera stops rolling, the lights are shut down, the mike is off, and you (or the reporter and crew) are out the door. Remember, you're on the record while on the interview scene.

One last tidbit. That red light on the TV camera can do funny things to people, like change their tone of voice or cause momentary laryngitis, twitches, sweaty palms or brow, or completely transform an otherwise sane individual into an actor "wannabe." Be yourself. After all, the reporter is interviewing you because you are who you are.

RADIO

Many tips about TV interviewing apply to radio as well. Here are a few salient points:

■ *While TV provides an image of you, radio relies solely on your voice.* You don't need pear-shaped tones to succeed, but you can make your voice more interesting by varying your pitch, tone and pacing. Modulate your voice, making it as expressive as possible. Listen to the professionals doing voice-overs on TV commercials. Don't confuse intensity with loudness; instead, stress your major points by emphasizing key words and phrases. Again, speak in sound bites.

■ *Radio demands brevity,* more so than TV. Your responses should be short and to the point. Speak deliberately and conversationally. Use anecdotes and examples to illustrate your main messages. Exude warmth, friendliness and sincerity.

■ *Be careful not to talk over or overlap the interviewer's question.* This makes it difficult for an editor to make clean cuts between the questions and your answers.

"Pithiness is a quality much admired by reporters. Convey your information clearly and succinctly in colorful language. And we love specific examples."

Peter Grier
Christian Science Monitor

"It never looks great in print to read 'Mr. Doe refused repeated requests for interviews.' While people sometimes say they can't speak on the subject, the reality is that they — or someone close to them — can speak on background to direct the reporter."

Ann Marie Squeo
The Wall Street Journal

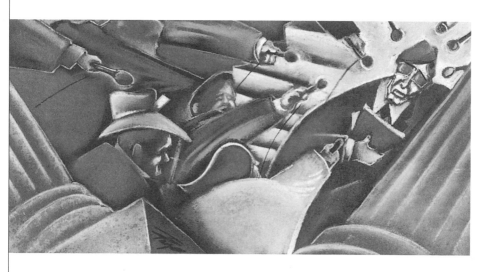

SPECIAL SITUATIONS

CHAPTER 4

This chapter takes a close look at several special situations: the hostile – or negative – interview, the ambush interview, international media, trade shows and other close encounters, and righting wrongs when you believe inaccurate reporting has occurred.

THE HOSTILE INTERVIEW

As mentioned previously, some interviews understandably may be controversial and perhaps even hostile. Keep in mind that the press after all is a business that sells a product. That may help you understand why reporters are attracted to conflict and controversy. Sensation sells. Like it or not, news is usually about something gone wrong. Remember, however, that if you want your views represented, you have to talk. When you don't, reporters will go to other sources or draw their own conclusions. Naturally, you will have to weigh the pros and cons and decide accordingly if you want to grant requests for such interviews. Beyond the techniques previously covered, here are some specific suggestions for neutralizing the negative.

■ *Practice, Practice, Practice:* The "murder board" approach we discussed earlier is a must in these situations. Make a list of the tough questions — *all* of the tough questions — reporters may ask. Together with your PR professionals, prepare your answers and put them on paper. Videotape your performance during a mock interview with colleagues, then have it reviewed and critiqued by unbiased, internal sources. Repeat this process until you are comfortable and prepared to respond to any question that may be asked.

■ *False Facts or Assumptions:* If asked a loaded question (one containing questionable facts or assumptions), don't repeat the false information. Simply correct the record by bridging to a positive point. For example, "How do you respond to critics on Capitol Hill who say the Boomerang missile is a 'turkey'?"

> **"***Denial or obfuscation of a problem that I know exists only makes matters worse. It just motivates me to find out what's really going on. Then you get a series of stories instead of one that lays it all out.***"**
>
> *Vargo Muradian*
> *Defense News*

Your response should be, "I disagree. The program has had its share of technical challenges, but we've turned the corner. The Boomerang is well on its way to meeting its operational objectives."

■ ***Putting Words in Your Mouth:*** Reporters may occasionally rephrase something you say and throw it back at you in a different context. Don't let them. Never repeat what the interviewer has said if it's not true or you don't agree. This only puts your comments on the record, which means they are available to your critics.

Alarms should sound if an interviewer asks, "So what you really mean is ..." or "So you really agree with the subcommittee's findings." If you don't and that is not your view, say so. State your opinion clearly and concisely to avoid misunderstanding. Also, be careful in accepting dubious facts or figures.

If you're not sure of the information, say so. Or if you have the correct information, provide it.

■ ***Painful But True:*** If the premise of a reporter's question is accurate, admit it, then bridge to your positive points. For example, if asked whether the Boomerang missile has had three test failures in a row, respond, "Yes, but let me put that in perspective. The Boomerang is not only the most advanced missile ever developed, but also the most thoroughly tested to date. It currently enjoys a success rate of 85 percent – the best rate of any comparable missile."

■ ***The "No-Win" Question:*** Occasionally, you may be asked a question that contains false choices. Don't fall into the trap. Instead, provide an accurate answer to the false choices presented. For example, if asked if the Boomerang test failures are due to poor design or problems with the software, you might reply,

> **66** *Obfuscation wastes everyone's time and always leaves me perplexed: Why sit down with a reporter if you won't answer any meaningful questions and provide some insight that couldn't otherwise be obtained by reading company press releases?* **99**
>
> **Ann Marie Squeo
> The Wall Street
> Journal**

"Analysis is still under way, so there is no answer at this point. However, based on overall test results to date, we are confident the Boomerang is meeting all test objectives."

■ *Multiple Questions at Once:* If a reporter poses several questions at once, choose the one that allows you to convey your positive message and ignore the others. You might reply, "You've asked me several questions; however, let me address what I believe is your most pertinent point."

THE AMBUSH INTERVIEW

You turn the corner and there they are: lights, cameras, microphones and reporters. Welcome to the ambush interview made famous by Mike Wallace and his "60 Minutes" crew. What do you do? What you *don't* do is start running and shouting, "No comment, no comment." Rather, attempt to establish order and control, and try to make the best of an awkward situation.

First, get the individual or group of reporters to settle down by indicating you will take their questions. Tell them you have a limited amount of time, but you'll try to be responsive. Make it clear you'll not answer any questions shouted at random, and you'll call on the individual to ask his or her question. Ask the reporters to identify themselves. After all, unless they are nationally known TV personalities, you probably don't know who or what media they represent. Don't proceed until you know who you're talking to.

If you're being crowded, ask them to step back and give you room. Remain calm, apply the lessons of *Media Isn't* ... and you'll do fine.

"*A good interview for me is when I walk away not only having learned some-thing I didn't know, but how that fits into the broader context of the story I'm working on.***"**

Vargo Muradian
Defense News

After a reasonable amount of time, tell the group you
have time for one more question. Answer it and scram.

INTERNATIONAL MEDIA

In this era of globalization, especially if your organization or company is engaged in international operations, you may occasionally have to interact with
international news media.

All the rules and recommendations outlined in this
book apply to media whether foreign or domestic.
But the obvious cultural differences call for some special rules of engagement with international media.

■ *Language:* Unless you have a good command of
the reporter's native language, the conversation will
be conducted in English. Even though your reporter
may be fluent, do not automatically assume that he

or she knows the language as well as you do and will understand all your points. Speak deliberately and slowly; use simple words; avoid colloquialisms; explain acronyms. When discussing complex or technical issues, pause occasionally to check whether all is understood. Invite the reporter to interrupt if some point escapes him or her.

■ *Culture:* Marked cultural differences, even among those nations referred to as the "Western" world, can influence perceptions. Try to get counsel from people familiar with the foreign environment you will be dealing with, especially regarding degrees of formality and other customs and traditions. (For instance, in German-speaking areas, it is unusual to use first names during an initial contact. Academic titles — Dr., Professor — are not skipped.) Anglo-Saxon directness sometimes clashes with Latin cultures, even more so with Arabic traditions. Humor, ususally not

"If you tell me something that you wish you hadn't said, correct it right away. I'll generally work with you, provided it isn't an evasion or complete reversal of what you said originally."

**Vargo Muradian
Defense News**

a problem with British and Dutch audiences, should be handled more carefully with the generally more formal German recipients and had best be waived entirely with Asian and Middle Eastern reporters.

■ *Politics:* Prevailing political attitudes toward the United States in your interviewer's country is another factor that can influence the exchange. This is also worth checking into before an interview takes place.

■ *Media Attitudes:* Finally, determining the editorial attitude of the media represented by your interviewer is even more important — and may take more time — than in the case of a domestic media encounter. Depending on the importance of the occasion, it may even be advisable to seek the counsel of the U.S. embassy or mission in the relevant country.

TRADE SHOWS
(AND OTHER CLOSE ENCOUNTERS)

If you have occasion to pull booth duty for your organization at a trade show, be alert to people standing within earshot, especially if you are talking to a customer. Many embarrassing news articles have resulted from overheard trade show conversations.

Chances are pretty good that at least one member of the media will happen by and strike up a conversation with you at your exhibit booth. Your company may have a policy covering such a contingency, and you should make sure you understand that policy before the event.

Determine ahead of time a basic explanation of your areas of responsibility within the booth, e.g., a set of brief, key points about your products and technologies,

" *We'll always set the record straight. But be careful about raising a ruckus, because rather than having something published one time and letting it die, you'll be exposing it to the public a second time.* **"**

Clarence A.
Robinson, Jr.
***SIGNAL** Magazine*

within the context of the graphic panels, data sheets and models on display. Then try to follow the suggestions presented here.

Since you're participating in a highly visible event open to the media, brushing off the reporter isn't a good idea. Rather, continue the conversation as an on-the-record interview and act accordingly. Be sure you know whom you're talking to. Although media members generally identify themselves as such, don't count on it. Be sure you know the name and affiliation of the reporter. Offer your business card for one in return. Then try to follow the advice presented here. It is also a good practice to brief your company or association PR contact about your encounter.

Similarly, if you are at a social event attended by media representatives, you are fair game. A good rule of thumb: Unless an agreement to the contrary is reached beforehand, consider any encounter with a reporter to be on the record. Avoid letting down your guard simply because you're not in a formal interview setting.

RIGHTING WRONGS

Sometimes, despite your best efforts, the story that results from your interview turns out wrong. Accept the likelihood that from time to time you are going to misspeak or be misquoted or that the essence of your meaning will be changed by a reporter. So what do you do? First, analyze the story. Try to be objective. If there are just a few inaccuracies, you probably can live with the story. However, if the report contains gross errors of fact that could spell trouble for your company and/or your program in the future, positive action is usually appropriate.

> **"***It is extremely important for spokespersons to handle controversies well. Don't lie or even fudge the truth. A reporter always is on guard against these tricks, and if you're caught, you'll never be trusted again.***"**
>
> **Larry Margasak**
> **Associated Press**

It is often helpful to get a second opinion, an objective view from someone who is not too close to the company and/or the subject at hand. In many cases, you don't have a problem. Remember, responding to a news report often creates what is known as a "second day" story or another forum to air the "dirty laundry" all over again. So think first before reacting. At times, it may be better to take the hit and let the story die.

If, on the other hand, the headline is downright misleading (by the way, don't blame the reporter, someone else writes the heads) or the article or broadcast report contains serious errors in fact, then it is not only appropriate, but your responsibility, to respond. With today's database retrieval systems and immediate online access, inaccurate reports left unchecked have the uncanny ability to resurface at the most inopportune time, such as during a budget hearing or a follow-on media interview.

- ***Correcting Erroneous Articles:*** The cardinal rule here is *don't argue with a man who buys ink by the barrel.* There will always be another edition or another broadcast.

First, make notes about the problems with the article. Remember, you must use specific facts to rebut an unfavorable story. Be sure they are based on fact and not simply a matter of interpretation or internal politics. Then, work with your PR staff to formulate the corrective strategy.

If, however, you're on your own, call and talk to the reporter. Don't go over his or her head, at least not initially. Don't be confrontational or irrational. Explain the problems in a calm, professional manner. Chances are the mistake will have been an honest one and can be easily fixed with a correction.

❝Hey, if we're wrong, we'll correct it. If we blow something, we'll fix it as quickly as we can. We can even do another story that says we really screwed up and here's what is right.❞

Rich Tuttle
Aerospace Daily

If you receive no satisfaction from the reporter, ask to speak to his or her boss immediately. Tell the reporter that as a matter of professional integrity, you intend to pursue the issue further with his or her superiors. Then do so.

You may also wish to write a letter to the editor for possible publication. Again, you need to carefully judge whether it is worth creating a second news forum for public consumption. If it's worth the shot, press on.

A few tips on writing your letter. First, make it brief, non-inflammatory and to the point. State your case positively and unemotionally. It's natural to feel personally frustrated by what you believe to be an unfair media report, but remember: Most bad press is over and forgotten within a few days *if it is handled professionally and positively.* Listen to your PR professionals and follow their advice.

The letters with the best chance of being published are those that add news value and/or bring a new dimension or perspective to the original story. Don't expect your letter to be published just because you wrote it or because your favorite ox may have been gored. Remember that guy who buys the ink.

■ *Correcting Erroneous Broadcast Reports:* Start by calling the error or problem to the reporter's attention and follow the general guidelines outlined on the previous page. If that doesn't work, move up the line to the station's news director until you are satisfied. If you act quickly, the correction may be made in time for the next newscast. Also, be prepared to provide a spokesperson to discuss the story on camera or in the studio if requested. And don't forget the popular radio call-in shows. If you have a comment to make and it has significant regional or national impact, make it.

> **"** *Please recognize that reporters are bombarded with pitches all day long and may not have time to respond to all of them. Don't be offended if you don't hear back from us. We're not trying to be rude, we're just strapped for time.* **"**
>
> *Karen Kaplan*
> *Los Angeles Times*

"If a company wants to share a 'success' story, it's important to remember we measure success largely by numbers. No numbers, no success, no story."

Jack Sweeney
Consulting Magazine

"Be careful about what you say. You're not talking to a judge or jury or the police. You don't have to tell everything. You can say, 'No comment' or 'That's none of your business.' Sometimes people are too open and can get themselves into deep trouble that way. No need to lay everything out."

Rich Tuttle
Aerospace Daily

THE VALUE-ADD OF PUBLIC RELATIONS

CHAPTER 5

Today more people, more entities, more groups and more inquiring minds are looking at ... you. And as they peer into your news releases, annual reports, brochures, stock price and past performance, they are asking serious questions about your net worth,

business practices and your social and ethical behavior.
All are basic questions that demand simple and easily understood answers.

CREATING BUSINESS VALUE

Too often, and for myriad professional and self-serving reasons, business enterprises have been prone to shy away from addressing critical issues "in the public domain." Instead, executives tend to default, allowing third-party interests — including the competition — to set the agenda for them. As a result, their agenda can become blurred or distorted as it is recorded and reported by the news media and ultimately interpreted by stakeholders, such as employees, clients, investors, financial and industry analysts, government regulators, competitors, and vendors and subcontractors.

Business today cannot ignore the news media. Some have tried, such as one industry president who once told me, "I control the media ... I don't talk to them." In our view, media's approach to covering business today is one of "proof or consequence." Either level with me, or pay the consequences.

The media today are concerned with reporting corporate responsibility along with corporate performance. When pieced together, these elements translate into a public image that is considered and acted upon by valued stakeholders. Consider the page one story in the March 24, 2002, *The Washington Post*, "Inside Andersen, A Fight for Image," reporting the frustration within the company following the Enron fiasco. According to the story, "[Andersen has] been encouraged by the private messages of support they have received ... but discouraged by how tough the public fight has been."

> **"** *Instead of trying to steer a reporter away from the truth, be honest enough to say you know something but can't discuss it. Then, have a good explanation for your refusal to answer. Better yet, be as expansive as possible and explain why you can't go further. None of this will make a reporter happy, but at least he or she won't think you're a snake. Honesty will leave the door open to cooperation later.* **"**
>
> **Larry Margasak**
> **Associated Press**

The public can be forgiving, however, candor and credibility are the only true pathways to timely acceptance. Any organization must ensure that its side of the story is accurately reported and ultimately understood by its valued publics. Survival is often at stake.

THE ESSENCE OF PR

So what is PR? First and foremost, it's an attitude. A proactive PR program sets you apart from the competition. It makes a compelling statement that your company recognizes its responsibility to articulate its position and net worth in the marketplace. It means you are not hesitant to be proactive. It means you are allowing your performance to undergo the most stringent of credibility tests: public opinion. In the simplest of terms, PR means winning and sustaining business. PR is taking credit for what you do. Contrary to some outdated views, there is nothing morally wrong in doing just that. Some executives feel uncomfortable stating "on the record" that they build the best product or offer the best value-added services. Why? If you don't believe it, why expect your customers to sign on?

PR is also crisis avoidance. It's being prepared for the troubled times – and yes, they will occur – when you have a delicate situation that may result in bad press. Which begs us to cite the usual senior management definition of good and bad press: Good press is when they say something nice about you, and bad press is when they say something you don't agree with. That said, management usually tends to pull back, shy away and avoid the embarrassment of any possible negative situation by just "letting it go away." Guess what, it won't.

It is during these times that a strong PR program, driven by a proactive media relations approach, can pay timely dividends. PR is not something only done in the sunlight. Rather, a savvy PR program requires your presence in the wind and rain, and often without an umbrella when the news is bad. This is the time to step up, face the truth and contribute positively to alleviating the situation. Sure, you may get a black eye for a day or two. But time will pass, another hot business story will hit page one, and – handled properly – your story will fade into history.

ELECTRONIC IMPLICATIONS

Addressing bad situations when they occur is especially important in today's Internet-savvy, media-driven society. Most reporters rely on the Internet and other computer-based databases to research stories. Once a news article appears, it becomes a permanent part of those databases, and the same information is often retrieved by other reporters and repeated in subsequent news accounts. If you don't take the time to set the record straight, you run the risk of experiencing continued bad press that could haunt you for years.

Remember, when you admit you've made a mistake, people — for the most part — tend to forget and move on. But when you lie and mislead, or remain silent, you make matters worse. It's an old lesson, but one that's still a hard sell in most of corporate America.

WORKING DEFINITION

Probably the most comprehensive definition of PR we've come across is that PR acts in the interest of those people, employees, customers, shareholders, communities, regulators and others, upon whom it depends for its success. These are the people who buy your products, enact legislation, refer potential customers, create stockholder value and, in the aggregate, play a major role in how your company is

"I look to work with individuals who understand the competitive and deadline pressures that are a part of our existence every day. In return, I'm hopeful these same individuals realize we know the difference between spin and substance, between information and news. After all, that's our business, news."

Mark Leibovich
The Washington Post

perceived. They must be informed and armed with the right information that will allow them to understand how your company is returning value to its stakeholders.

While the news media should not be official members of this list, they should at least be considered for associate membership. The lesson here is to conduct your affairs mindful of the media and what media exposure might mean to the situation at hand.

INVOLVEMENT IS KEY

PR practitioners must be positioned as informed and involved members of any organization's senior management staff. To be positioned elsewhere is only paying lip service to the function. PR must be seated at the management table on a regular basis in order to protect that fickle and often mercurial asset known as reputation. In so doing, PR has the daily responsibility to keep its eyes, ears and fingers firmly on the pulse of those communities where an organization maintains a presence.

Too often, PR is perceived and used as an 11th-hour panacea expected to deliver informed and immediate counsel even if not involved in the strategy to address the situation at hand. Unfortunately, it just doesn't work this way. PR must be involved from the start, not just when you encounter trouble, but on an ongoing basis, just like the chief financial officer and general counsel. Like it or not, PR is often the single corporate entity that is specifically tasked to step back and provide a "devil's advocate" or "alter ego" point of view. Why are we laying off 50 employees the day before Thanksgiving? Or, why aren't we keeping our employees informed about this action that will ultimately affect them?

> **"Don't be afraid to pitch a story via e-mail. That way I can concentrate on what you're saying when I'm not on deadline or focused on another subject. Talking on the phone isn't necessary to get me interested in a story."**
>
> *Karen Kaplan*
> *Los Angeles Times*

The key to PR is early involvement, often and always. PR practitioners understand that awareness and visibility can lead to understanding and support, which ultimately means profitability — the true bottom-line objective.

Our message: Get PR out in the open. Make it a visible and involved part of your management processes, not just solely your publicity agent. The operative word here is visible. If it is perceived that PR is only a last-minute, rainy-day solution, that's the way it's going to be treated and recognized by employees and media alike. But if PR is perceived as a mainline, integral part of the management process, supported at the highest levels of senior management, then you are positioned for success.

CHAPTER 6

FROM THE EDITOR'S DESK
By Richard C. Barnard
Former Vice President, Executive Editor, Defense News

Those who regularly complain that reporters know

next to nothing about them and their industry will

not spend 10 minutes trying to understand the press.

These are often the same people who are so busy running and ducking that they have no time to work with the media to capitalize on the genuine accomplishments of their companies.

Yet others are consistently successful at talking with reporters and getting their points of view into headlines and in front of the various publics they need to reach. What is the difference between those who get their message across and those who crash and burn? In my considerable years of covering military and aerospace issues, I have noticed that those companies and individuals who frequently succeed share some of the same characteristics and practices.

Here, listed in no particular order, are a few observations gleaned from my regular contacts with some of the best news sources in government and industry.

Understand how reporters view your company. In their eyes, you work for a public organization that spends millions of public dollars on costly public machines. Reporters believe you are obligated to answer questions about your work.

Be realistic. Do not expect the press to regularly gush about your hardware and innovations or take your company's press releases and rush them to print. The job of reporters is to cover the news, not form a cheering section for industry or government. Your objective should be to get what you deserve. The press is obliged to report news developments fairly and with reasonable balance. Reporters should accurately convey your comments and the context in which you made them.

Do not use that favorite industry standby: "No comment." In fact, that is a comment. Based on years of experience, the press will conclude that you have something to hide. Typically, industry is delighted to comment when things are going well.

Be wary of those who mouth the pat phrase, "The press never tells our side." That is classic excuse-making by people who would rather sit on their rumps than cultivate a relationship with the media.

Tell it like it is. Don't equivocate and don't rationalize your way into telling an untruth. The reporter will walk away from the interview with two stories instead of one. There will be times when the best answer you can give the press is, "We made a mistake, and the steps we are taking to correct it are ... ."

Never forget that dealing with the press is not a one-way street. Reporters need you. The aerospace and defense industries, for example, are tough beats to cover. The issues are complex, deadlines are short and most reporters work hard to get the story straight. One of the best sources I ever had spent hours telling me about antisubmarine warfare. I never wrote a story about the way sound travels in water, but his tutorials about it helped me to understand the broader issues. Another source took me on a long, winding trip from industry through the Congress and into the White House. It lasted for years. Along the way, I came to understand better than most how Washington really works. A third source opened the door to the Pentagon's black world.

These people weren't talking to me just to be nice. They wanted their views reported. They wanted to

have a hand in setting the political agenda. They
wanted to send messages to a variety of publics in
the United States and abroad.

Did I listen to them? You bet. And I also tried to
talk to those with opposing views. The point is that
those who truly understand reporters' hunger for
information rarely have a hard time getting access
to the press.

The fruitful conversations with each of my best
sources began to take place only after a few routine
encounters. I came to know them as knowledgeable,
straightforward people who weren't involved in
Washington's cottage industry: disinformation.

I hope they came to know me as a seasoned reporter
without a secondary agenda, one who knew his stuff
and could be relied upon not to violate a confidence.

That brings me to my final observation: The best press relations are simply good human relations. Get to know the reporters who cover your industry. There are lots of good ones out there. Find them, and give them a chance to know you. You don't have to be pals or golfing buddies. But there should be a give-and-take relationship based on the mutual understanding that your jobs and your objectives often converge.

FROM THE VETERAN NEWSMAN
By Howard Banks
Former Assistant Managing Editor, Forbes Magazine

Many years ago, as I was passing through New York on my way back to England, I called Willis Player, then vice president of public relations for Pan Am and the doyen of the airline industry communicators. "Come to lunch," he said.

Also present in the dining room at the top of the Pan Am building, to my surprise, was Bill Seawell, then chairman and CEO, who filled my head with all sorts of stuff. Interesting stuff, about which I wrote a piece for *The Economist,* my employer at the time. No sooner had it appeared than Will called from New York.

"Nice piece," he said, "but why on earth did you say ...?" I can't recall what the offending words were, but they had seriously frosted Seawell. They were not important words and formed part of a smart-aleck paragraph that connected two separate elements of the Seawell story. Any offense given was entirely unintentional — if I intend to stick it to someone, they usually can tell.

A week or two later, Will called again, saying he would be in London and asking if we could have lunch. I agreed, even if it meant moving a few things around in the diary, since I felt just a bit guilty about getting Will into hot water with his boss. As lunch was ending, Will dropped into the conversation that he liked it when journalists made the kind of "mistake" (well, what he saw as a mistake) that I had made. Reason? "I just got three hours of your time to talk about the business."

What do I take from this, other than the fact that lunch used to be a much more leisurely affair? An almost universal difference in the behavior of top PR people these days. Will was ready, even keen, to pass on his substantial knowledge about the airline business and the industry's main suppliers (aircraft, engines, airports and the rest). Yes, it was all on background, but there was no discernible company-focused spin going on. He believed that getting better-informed coverage would benefit Pan Am, even if only indirectly.

These days, it is hard to get many top PR people — those one might hope are reasonably well informed about what is going on in their industry — to talk generally about their sector. Most comments made about other companies are negative, an attempt to show the rival in a bad light. Result? A lack of corporate input to help journalists broaden their understanding of what drives business. This, it seems to me, inevitably increases the chance of stories containing errors or distortions, which is a factor behind the mostly antagonistic relationship that now exists between press and business.

My advice? PR executives should follow Will's example and share in-depth background information about their industry with trusted members of the press. Better informed reporters will ultimately, if indirectly, benefit your industry.

FROM THE PR TRENCHES

Much can be stated, studied and debated about the practice of public relations. But the greatest lessons are learned when the press calls and the pressure is on. What follows is a true account as written by our colleague and friend, Robert T. Gilbert, a public relations professional in the information technology industry.

MANAGER'S JOURNAL: WHAT TO DO WHEN THE PRESS CALLS

By Robert T. Gilbert
PR Professional

Put yourself in this situation, based entirely on fact: A reporter from a major business publication calls to say she's doing a story about the contraction in your industry, especially as experienced by "second-tier" companies like yours. She's been told your financial results are way down. Further, she's heard from your competitors that, owing to a scandal, you've laid off a sizable group of people. She'd like to talk to your CEO today.

Welcome to the world of corporate public relations, where hardly anybody who doesn't scent blood is interested in you. PR is the contact sport of corporate communications, adversarial by the very nature of its two opposing goals: the media's relentless search for bad news versus companies' efforts to get out the good.

In our case, the reporter had drawn the worst possible interpretation from a few hard kernels of truth. As head of PR for your company, what would you do? Decline to comment? Read her some glowing paragraphs out of the marketing literature? Threaten to sue for libel?

Actually, your only real option is to play ball. It's the only way you have to affect the story's outcome, or at least soften its premise. If the facts are on your side, you can provide counterbalancing data and opinion, as well as correct misinformation. If you are lucky enough to be dealing with an experienced reporter who's not too harassed by a deadline, you can change the tenor of the story.

Most important, you have to persuade your top executives to carry the ball, balancing between candor and prudence, because reporters never want to quote the PR guy. (My CEO said he found the whole experience "depressing.")

In dealing with reporters, it helps to understand their motivation and how they work. Reporters are remarkably similar in their desire to, as Mr. Dooley's phrase goes, comfort the afflicted and afflict the comfortable. (Hence a perennial favorite is the story about inflated CEO pay.) Of course, reporters also want to get the story first. They approach a story from a point of view based on what they know. They have an idea of how they're going to write the story, but they're supposed to find out what's really going on. In the memorable words of Ben Bradlee, former executive editor of *The Washington Post,* reporters don't write "the truth," they interpret "what we know and what people tell us."

This means you have to tell them something. If you can show a good reporter that his facts aren't facts at all, or that the way he's interpreting them adds up to an erroneous impression, he will adjust the story. This isn't guaranteed: Bad or sloppy reporters just fill in the blanks of a preconceived story line, and editors and rewrite people can give an article a cynical edge the reporter didn't intend.

And even if you're dealing with the best reporters, you should expect to get dinged in any story about your company. One of the fundamentals of serious business reporting is to eliminate "puffery" in favor of "balance." Balance comes from your competitors, industry analysts, stock watchers and other critics, who have an interest in being quoted – and don't usually get quoted unless the comment is both color-ful and negative. In my experience, executives love "balance" in stories about their competitors but are deeply offended by it in stories about their own companies.

On the whole and over time, your company usually gets the publicity it deserves. But it can be a bumpy ride, because news is only "news" if it's different from the last story. This causes a sort of pendulum effect on coverage. For example, back in the 1980s, when *Time* magazine said IBM was nearly as important an organization as the Vatican, the company's PR people instantly knew that the next set of stories would have to be contrarian. This oscillation is especially noticeable in the auto industry, where coverage swings between glowing product launches and recalls or sales slumps.

For those who would hire PR people, and those who would enter the occupation, here are a few lessons:

- If you crave publicity for your company, remember the old law about getting what you want. Being covered by reporters means being subjected to intensely skeptical scrutiny.

- Tell the truth. Journalists are going to find out anyway, and your integrity is on the line. This doesn't, however, mean volunteering information without being asked. Nor should you shy from telling a reporter something isn't any of his business, when it isn't. Your point of view should be positive in all this, to apply your own "balance." If the water is at midpoint, reporters tend to write that "the glass is half empty, and draining." Your position should be that it's "half full and rising."

- For those who aspire to (or blunder into) PR, know that personal anonymity is the rule. Only during a pinch do powerful businessmen view PR people as trusted counselors. Nor can you count on long-lasting relationships with members of the media. Often, you're in a position of trying to pitch the kind of "good news" stories that don't win Pulitzers. (For example, I cannot for the life of me get any business reporter interested in the fact my company donated $4.6 million of time and expenses to a major city's school system.) Your real value to the media comes from responding quickly to requests for information, having genuine industry knowledge and, especially, getting the right executive on the line, quickly.

The final lesson of PR is that the game is mostly one-sided. Returning to the opening example, the reporter's story eventually appeared, and we got slammed as expected. Yet it could have been much worse. The most outrageous assertions didn't make it. The reference to our company was buried and mercifully brief. And the reporter gave a fair hearing to our point of view. Because we played ball, we came through with a few grass stains but no serious injuries.

This account was first published as a Manager's Journal in The Wall Street Journal *on June 17, 1996, and is reprinted here with permission of* The Wall Street Journal, *copyright 1996, Dow Jones & Company, Inc.*

AUTHORS' FOOTNOTE

Dealing with the media means dealing with perceptions, controversy and change. American industry makes news every day. Reporting that mammoth story is the responsibility of the media. Conveying perceptions through the filters of reporters, editors and producers to remain competitive in a global market may be risky but, in our opinion, is well worth the rewards. Remember, visibility and awareness can equal understanding and support. Stated differently: What people understand, they tend to trust; what they trust, they may support.

In dealing with the news media, some would rather curse the darkness than light a candle. The industry president referred to earlier who claimed he controlled the media by not talking to them did have a strategy, but one that was totally ineffective and noncompetitive.

Declaring war on the media has long been a game — a game you can't win. In fact, it's one you shouldn't even play. Sure, the judicial system is available for those with irreconcilable differences; however, business and the media have no choice but to live with each other. Our relationship is best described as adversarial, but that's the way it should be. That's why freedom of the press is, and will always remain, one of the sustaining principles of this great nation.

- View every interview as an opportunity to establish your points about the issue at hand or your business relationship with that issue.

- Remember the cardinal rules: If you don't want it in print or on the air, don't say it, and engage brain before putting mouth in gear.

- The three most important words in getting ready for a media interview are preparation, preparation and preparation.

- Have an agenda: What are your main points?

- Stick to your area of expertise.

- Anticipate the tough questions and prepare your answers ahead of time.

- Practice before a "murder board."

- Establish, define and agree upon ground rules before an interview begins.

- Accentuate the positive, eliminate the negative. Try to control the interview.

- Answer all questions briefly and truth-fully. Put your conclusions first. If you don't know the answer, say so. Offer to find out. Follow through quickly.

- Illustrate your answers with specific examples, colorful language and meaty quotes.

- Remember, the interview isn't over until it's over. Watch what you say any time a reporter is present, especially during informal situations.

- Remember, at all times you are speaking as a representative of your company, association or business entity.

DO ...

👍 Consult with your PR staff before proceeding if you are contacted directly by a member of the news media.

👍 Be accessible to and truthful with the media.

👍 Coordinate with your management and government customer/prime contractor (if applicable) before you agree to an interview.

👍 Prepare for all media interviews.

👍 Discuss only those activities within your area of expertise, knowledge and responsibility.

👍 Establish your agenda of three to five points and work them in at every opportunity.

👍 Anticipate questions, particularly the tough ones, and plan your answers in advance.

👍 Tape-record your interview.

👍 Establish, define and agree to ground rules at the outset.

DO ...

- Use simple, direct sentences. Be positive.
- Keep your cool and maintain your professionalism at all times.
- Answer the question and only the question.
- Assume media are present if you are participating or presenting in a public meeting.

DON'T ...

▶ Use jargon, acronyms or highly technical terms.

▶ Volunteer information, unless it supports one or more of your message points.

▶ Let a reporter put words in your mouth. Agree only if the facts and figures are true.

▶ Answer hypothetical (what-if) questions, unless the information supports your strategy.

▶ Stonewall, lie, evade or bluff. If you can't answer a question, say why: "That's classified," or "That's company proprietary" or "I don't know."

▶ Stray from the farm. Address only those issues in your area of competence and responsibility.

▶ Tell a reporter something, then add, "That's off the record." It isn't.

▶ Switch ground rules during the interview.

▶ Try to be cute. It usually will backfire. News media representatives do this for a living; you don't.

▶ Get too chummy or too formal. Remember, it's an adversarial relationship.

DON'T ...

⊘ Ask a reporter to let you review his or her story prior to publication.

⊘ Call a reporter to ask his or her news source for a particular story.

⊘ Ignore media deadlines.

⊘ Promise to provide an answer or information and not follow through.

⊘ Ask the reporter to send you a clipping or TV tape when a story is published or aired.

⊘ Ask your PR staff to set up press interviews or a news conference when you have no real news to report.

⊘ Threaten to pull advertising from a publication because it published a negative story.

⊘ Believe there is a direct link between the amount of advertising you place and how much editorial coverage you will receive from that publication or news outlet.

⊘ Make yourself available to the media only when there is good news.

DON'T ...

- ⊘ View editorial coverage as free advertising.

- ⊘ Assume that because an interview took place, a story or news report will appear.

- ⊘ View the media as freeloaders. Most media representatives prefer to pay their own way to ensure their continued objectivity and professionalism.

- ⊘ Keep your professional PR staff in the dark on possible newsworthy or negative issues.

- ⊘ Let your legal department dictate PR or media relations policy.

APPENDIX D

Checklist for TV

Appearances

MEN AND WOMEN

- Dress conservatively. Solid colors are preferred; wear dark shoes.
- Avoid stripes, checks, small prints or patterned fabrics.
- Wear light-colored shirts or blouses.
- Wear glasses if you need them, but tilt them down slightly to eliminate any glare from the lights.
- Remove company badges and pens or pencils from pockets.
- Ensure that briefcases, purses, etc., are out of camera range.

MEN

- Wear long-sleeved shirts, gray or light blue preferred. Avoid bright white shirts.
- Be sure your suit or coat and trousers are freshly pressed.
- Wear a conservative tie.
- For a sit-down interview, wear over-the-calf socks.

- Shave before you go to the studio regardless of time of day.
- If it's a sit-down interview, unbutton your coat.
- Don't wear a vest.

WOMEN

- Wear makeup appropriate for the business office.
- Jewelry is fine, but avoid large, bright pieces that may flare under studio lights.
- Wear solid, medium-colored suits or dresses. Make sure your knees are covered when you sit down.

Without fear of offending a particular late-night TV host, the following are our Top 10 Tenets of Practical Public Relations. The list represents a collection of comments and counsel from some of the finest pros in the business, plus some firsthand lessons learned working the PR trenches.

10 Lawyers tell you what you must do; public relations tells you what you should do.

9 Tell it like it is.

8 Never mind what is, but what appears to be is.

7 Silence is not golden; stand up and be counted.

6 Don't argue with somebody who buys ink by the barrel.

5 Ask why, not how.

4 Serve as devil's advocate and alter ego for management.

3 Seek to influence policy, not make it.

2 Remember: Public opinion is the final arbiter.

1 Assume the role of the CRO — Corporate Reputation Officer.

APPENDIX E

Top 10 Tenets of Practical Public Relations

APPENDIX F

Contributors

ABOUT THE AUTHORS

David J. Shea and John F. Gulick, APR, are career public relations professionals who both began their professional careers as information officers in the United States Air Force. As retired USAF officers, they continue their long-standing support and affiliation with the career field as active members of the Air Force Public Affairs Alumni Association.

Shea is director, Media Relations, Raytheon Company, in Washington, D.C. He concluded a 29-year Air Force career in 1988 when he joined the former Hughes Aircraft Company. In his final military assignment, he was the Pentagon's director of defense information, responsible for the daily news operations of the Department of Defense. He holds a bachelor's degree in communication arts from Fordham University and a master's degree in mass communications from the University of Denver. He and his wife Mary are the parents of three daughters and live in northern Virginia.

Gulick started his own PR and media consulting practice in April 2002 after serving 10 years as a director of communications with Computer Sciences Corporation in Falls Church, Va., and San Diego, Calif. Prior to his CSC tenure, he was a director with COMSAT Corporation, Grumman Corporation and the Fairchild Republic Co. He also founded and operated Gulick Public Relations, Inc., an advertising and PR agency in Fort Walton Beach, Fla. During a

20-year Air Force career, he performed in a number of key public affairs positions, primarily in support of USAF research, development and acquisition activities.

Gulick holds a bachelor's degree in journalism from Temple University and a master's degree in public relations from The American University. He and his wife Lynn have two children and two grandchildren and live in northern Virginia. He is accredited in public relations by the Public Relations Society of America.